BIRDS

in Words and Images

by Barbara Freedman-De Vito

Baby Bird Productions

Copyright
© 2019
Barbara G. Freedman-De Vito

Baby Bird Productions
www.babybirdproductions.com

AN INTRODUCTION TO BIRDS

Yes, birds beguile us, charm, amuse,
So here are some you may peruse.

These birds were drawn with love and care,
And now these birds are here to share.

I've chosen many different types,
Picked birds of many different stripes,

So some are flightless, others soaring,
Some are common, but never boring.

While some may be much more exotic,
Perhaps they're even quite hypnotic.

There's arctic and there's tropical,
From simple to quite optical.

The large and, sure enough, the small,
I've tried hard to include them all.

Each picture comes with its own verse
Which is not great, but could be worse.

I hope you will enjoy the art
Because these birds all stole my heart.

THE KESTREL

A raptor true,
In reddish brown
With blackish spots,
An earth tone gown.

A hunting bird
Up in the skies,
You hover there,
Use such sharp eyes.

Then down you zoom
To catch your prey
And live to see
Another day.

Or perch upon
A tree or pole,
Then pounce upon
A mouse or vole.

You live in holes
In cliffs or trees
Or inside barns -
In all of these,

But hunt in heath
Or open field,
Or shrub or marsh,
See what they yield.

The poets say
You symbolize
All nature's strength,
Despite your size.

Your majesty
And quiet grace
Bring dignity
To this wild place.

THE
KESTREL

THE PARAKEET

Your beak is stout
And used to shout,
Or peck at fruit,
Or climb about.

Australian soul,
Like kangaroo,
Small parrot breed
Called budgie, too.

You play your games,
You sing your song,
Amuse yourself
The whole day long,

Out in the wild
You nest in trees
And live in flocks
And ride the breeze.

And as you do,
Amuse us all,
With bobbing head
Or standing tall.

Petit in size,
Your pretty wings,
Blues, yellows, greens,
Can brighten scenes.

Now beat your wings,
Now perch, now dance,
And if I can,
I'll catch a glance.

A funny clown,
Despite your grace,
Black stripes and dots
Adorn your face.

THE
PARAKEET

THE CARDINAL

Your jaunty red
Well-pointed crest
Sure makes you look
Your very best.

And with that mask
Upon your face,
I'd pick you out
In any place.

You're truly named
For cardinals' caps,
And long red robes
Worn by those chaps.

You live in woods
And gardens, too,
But swamps and shrubs
Will also do.

You mate for life
And sing duets,
And build your nests
And fight off threats.

I love to hear
You sing your song,
A whistled tune.
Your voice is strong.

I love to watch
You eat the seeds
That I put out
To serve your needs.

So many states
Have chosen you
To be state bird,
A fine choice, too.

THE
CARDINAL

THE ANHINGA

Called water turkey,
    snakebird, darter,
    and anhinga, too,
Although you go
    by many names
    to thine own self you're true.

You're shiny black
    with hints of green,
    some feathers blackish-blue,
Pale purple bits
    on neck and back,
    of such a pretty hue.

A yellow shade
    on feet and bill
    to round your image out,
You're long and thin,
    majestic bird,
    of that there is no doubt.

You love to swim
    in warmer climes,
    just head and neck protrude,
Appearing like
    a prowling snake
    who's ready to intrude.

Your long slim bill
    is critical
    in spearing fish you want.
To stay alive
    that's how you hunt,
    in shallows that you haunt.

Your feathers are
    not watertight;
    that helps you not to float.
You stay beneath
    the water more,
    just like a capsized boat.

And if you fly
    with wings still wet,
    you flap to no avail,
And seem to skip
    your way across
    the water like a sail.

To dry your wings
    you spread them out
    while in the open air.
Warm sunshine really
    works a treat.
    I love to watch you there.

You often hunt
    for food in groups
    with such a lovely name,
Called "kettles of
    anhinga," wow !
    Now that's a claim to fame !

THE
ANHINGA

THE HUMMINGBIRD

Such tiny sprites
Who greet the night
And flit about
In dusky light

Like fairy folk
Among the flowers,
I watch entranced
For hours and hours.

I've seen you all
Around a bower,
Buzz back and forth
And never cower.

Sip nectar there
Without a care,
Use slender beak
And drink your share.

With rapid wings
You beat the air,
Defy all laws
Existing there.

You catch the light
In sparkling hues,
In shades of purple,
Reds and blues.

You've such a sheen,
An iridescence.
I'm in awe when
In your presence.

Your magic glows
And makes me smile.
Please let me watch
You for a while.

THE
HUMMINGBIRD

THE PENGUIN

Why penguins are so popular
Is not so hard to see :
Your cuteness,
   all in black and white,
Your antics in the sea.

Your colors are no accident,
They play a vital role :
Give camouflage
   to swimming birds
In water - that's the goal.

Seen from above
   your blackened backs
Blend in with shadowy bays.
Seen from below
   your whiteness hides
You in the sunlight's rays.

Though clumsy movers
   on dry land
Who really cannot fly,
Adapted to the watery depths
You "fly" as you swim by.

For ancient wings
   evolved with time
To flippers that now grow,
And buoyant plumage
   insulates
From cold and wet below.

On land you slide across the ice
On bellies, that saves time,
Or waddle slowly back and forth
And jump on rocky rime.

You live in great big colonies,
Protect your eggs from cold
By hiding them upon your feet
Beneath a feathery fold.

So many species now exist
From "fairy penguin" breeds
To "emperor penguins"
   of great size
With larger spacial needs.

And so I ask,
   what's not to love ?
You have such great appeal,
So let's protect your habitat,
Protect it with great zeal.

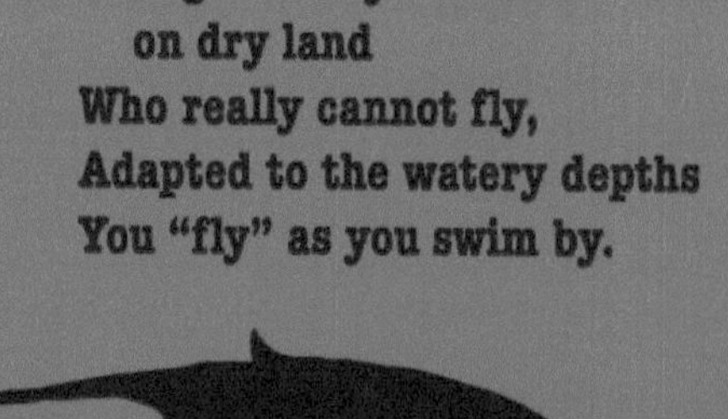

THE
CHINSTRAP PENGUIN

THE TOUCAN

A funny head
By any norm –
Proportions off,
Ungainly form.

In contrast to
Your blackened coat,
So sleek and smooth,
Of which you gloat.

A rainbow lives
Upon your face,
A comic beak that's
Lacking grace.

In truth that bill
Can serve you well.
It grabs at fruit,
Your thirst to quell.

You fence with it,
Intimidate,
Claim holes in trees
Others excavate.

Small flocks make up
Your neighborhoods,
So sociable
Out in the woods.

From Mexico to
Argentina,
And in-between,
Some folks have seen ya.

A constellation
Bears your name.
It's called "Tucana"
And spreads your fame.

THE
TOUCAN

THE PELICAN

Amusing bird
    of awkward shape,
Untamed and flying free,
What luck to spot
    you in the wild.
You're such a thrill to see.

Mythology has
    sung your praise,
From Egypt, up to now,
As symbol of
    an afterlife,
Or on a great ship's bow.

Your name comes from
    an old Greek word.
It comes from "pelekan."
Quite simply put,
    your name means "axe."
Go figure, if you can.

You haunt the coast
    and inland, too,
And travel in
    large flocks.
You roost upon
    a sandy beach,
Are seen among
    the docks.

You capture fish
    in your large bill,
Your pouch, a holding tank.
Then drain the water,
    swallow hard,
Out on the outer bank.

You soar on thermals
    high above,
Ten thousand feet or more,
And travel many
    miles each day
To feed on some new shore.

I've seen you in
    a slate gray sky,
Skim over glassy seas,
You seem a
    prehistoric sight,
A shadow on the breeze.

The world would be
    a poorer place
Without you
    by the shore.
A striking relic
    of the past
        And, oh, you're so
        much more.

THE
PELICAN

THE BLUE JAY

I thought I saw a flash of blue -
A bird rose in the air,
Slow flyer, graceful, lovely, too,
A bird who shows such flair.

A new world bird who's quite at home
In woodland and in town,
Your noisy banter make me think
I've found a blue-clad clown.

Distinctive blue, with bars of black,
Pale face and undersides,
A collared neck, black bill and legs,
And jaunty crest, besides.

That crest moves up when you are riled,
Responds to each new mood.
It bristles out when you are scared,
Lies flat when nibbling food.

You love to eat both seeds and nuts.
Soft fruit makes quite a snack.
You'll even hide a nut or two,
Then later take it back.

You'll build a nest shaped like a cup,
Alongside with your mate.
Soon colored eggs appear within,
Hatch at a later date.

Your jay bird genus comes from Greek,
"Blue chatterer," in fact,
And this because you love to talk,
Although you lack much tact.

You'll challenge all who threaten you,
Or who approach your nest,
And chase them off, harass them, too,
Both cat and hawk you'll best.

You'll scold them in your strident voice
Until they take the hint.
You'll drive them off and dive at them,
Black eyes reveal a glint.

Let's show respect when we catch sight
Or hear your raucous call.
Although you're common in our yards,
You're special, after all !

THE
BLUE JAY

THE FLAMINGO

It's sad that you've
Become clichés,
Adorning lawns
In neon shades.

Reality's
Another tale,
Of water bird
With hot pink tail.

In ancient times,
Egyptian lore
Said you were Ra,
And watched you soar.

From Portuguese,
Your pretty name
Means you're the color
Of a flame,

And when you eat
And are well-fed,
You brighten more,
To shades of red.

That helps you to
Attract a mate,
To share your life,
Not just one date.

To find your food,
You stamp your feet.
That stirs the mud
And works a treat.

You like to stand
On just one leg,
So long and thin,
A slender peg.

As wading birds
In giant flocks,
Make waves of pink,
As each bird walks.

So don't let people
Put you down,
With grace and charm,
You're no one's clown.

THE
FLAMINGO

THE PIGEON

Columbidae is what you are.
You're known as rock doves, too.
Monogamy, that is your creed.
You love to bill and coo.

Both males and females
    raise your young.
You're found all 'round the earth,
From cliffs to city skyscrapers,
Wherever you give birth.

You bob your head
    to fix your gaze.
You fly with strength and grace,
Maneuver sharply in the air.
Some put you in a race.

Your homing instincts
    have been used
By men in times of war
To carry vital messages,
As over fields you'd soar.

Gregarious, granivorous,
You breed the whole year through.
Your shiny green and purple necks
Make you real beauties, too.

You know you are my favorite birds,
For many I have met.
I've rescued you and cared for you,
And one became a pet.

Well, some were saved
    from being forced
To breed squabs raised for meat,
And one was saved
    from subway tracks,
And that was no mean feat !

One orphaned bird became a pet,
Because he could not fly.
He lived with us for years and years,
Gave joy each day gone by.

Your gentle spirits, friendliness,
And trusting hearts ring true.
For every pigeon I have known,
I've made this book for you.

THE
PIGEON

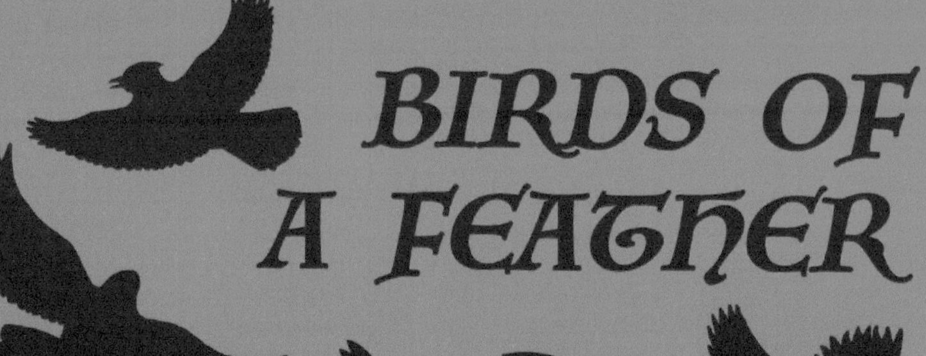

BIRDS OF A FEATHER

From Audubon to Big Bird,
The Maltese Falcon, too,
From Tweetie Pie
   to Donald Duck,
And doves that bill and coo,

Birds thrive in modern culture.
They have such great appeal.
Why do we love
   and need them so ?
I'll answer this by feel.

Well, first there is their beauty,
Their graceful silhouettes,
Majestic, big
   bald eagles
To little alouettes.

Next, they have such colors,
And iridescent sheen,
From hummingbirds
   to humble crows,
Enhancing every scene.

Of course, we love their singing,
Each voice is quite unique,
From simple chants
   to complex songs,
And some can even speak !

Birds also symbolize some things
We wish life held in store :
A phoenix rises
   from the ash,
A dove of peace ends war.

But most of all we love their flight
And wish that we could fly.
Who hasn't wished
   to join them
In a race across the sky ?

In wintry parks, at feeders,
In open flight, at rest,
Or singing in
   a summer tree,
Or feeding chicks in nest,

Birds add enrichment to our lives.
Birds touch us to our core.
From zooming swifts
   to ostriches,
They help our spirits soar.

THE
END

Barbara also writes and
illustrates original picture books
for children (each with a bonus
draw and tell story included at
the end of the book). To find these,
plus her Draw and Tell Story
collections, please visit
amazon.com or amazon.co.uk
(or your favorite jobber)
and look for :

Barbara Freedman-De Vito

For bird art prints, T-shirts and other
clothing and gift items for the entire family,
all decorated with Barbara's designs,
plus free activities for children and teachers,
and many free informative articles for parents,
please visit Barbara's website at :

www.babybirdproductions.com